So What
Do I Do
Now?

So What Do I Do Now?

A Thought-Filled Guide to Retirement

Jeanne Taylor McClellan

SO WHAT DO I DO NOW?
A THOUGHT-FILLED GUIDE TO RETIREMENT

iUniverse books may be ordered through booksellers or by contacting:

iUniverse
1663 Liberty Drive
Bloomington, IN 47403
www.iuniverse.com
844-349-9409

ISBN: 978-1-6632-1850-6 (sc)
ISBN: 978-1-6632-1851-3 (e)

Library of Congress Control Number: 2021903273

Print information available on the last page.

iUniverse rev. date: 02/22/2021

To my husband

Our adventures continue …

Contents

Part IV: Arranging
The Practical Side of Life

Preface

This book has taken some time (read *years*) to put together. Interestingly enough, my life got interrupted with my own retirement. Over the years as I have lived this journey each chapter has taken on a life of its own.

It all began with a conversation with my husband. We were sitting on our deck enjoying the backyard view of the fruit trees and productive vegetable gardens my husband had put over twenty-six years of effort and love into designing, developing, and maintaining on this acre. He enjoyed every minute of the work and the evening views.

It was a lovely late-spring evening, and we were considering where our life together was going. The kids were all well on their own. Our grandchildren were in college and/or on their way. We felt settled into a life of part-time work (translate that to working on our own schedule), travel, and enjoying our life path. We realized that the house was now too big for just the two of us and its upkeep was taking more time and energy than we wanted to expend. It appeared that this road we were traveling together had an unexpected turn coming up.

As a couple, we have always embraced whatever life offered us, so we explored, verbally, what our next adventure would be. We weighed our various options: staying put, hiring house help to take over the more strenuous yard work, or finding a smaller house. Remember this was just a conversation!

Then our life's journey took a sharp turn in the form of family death, illness, and general growing pains.

We realized that the life we were enjoying with no end in sight could be taken away without any warning. Time had become our constant enemy. As my husband says, "We go to bed on Sunday night and wake up Friday morning." Life was moving faster than we had anticipated. We watched as our friends, some older and some younger, made the decision that we now faced. We were at a crossroads. Should we stay on our current path or take a new road? We were facing our next adventure.

For the past several years, my closest friends had been asking me, "When are you going to retire?" They all had retired years before and were concerned that I was working too hard and avoiding this next stage of my life. I had no answer for them. In fact, I found the question frightening in many ways.

The picture of retirement that I had in my head was of me sitting on a porch in a rocking chair enjoying an adult beverage as the water of a serene lake/river/ocean (you know, something calming) flowed along and the birds sang and a breeze blew gently through my hair. It was an idyllic picture like the canvas photos you see in the tourist shops in every vacation spot you've ever visited. Ahhhh …

The problem was that as much as that picture oozed of serenity and contentment it was not my vision. My vision was one of financial insecurity (close to panic!) and fear of terminal boredom (close to terror!). After all, how could I be sure I'd be able to retire financially, physical, and emotionally?? How would I live?? And most importantly, *what would I do*?

I saw my friends happy and content in their retired life—almost ecstatically so. I knew there had to be a middle ground between their ecstasy and my panic. I wanted to find that. I had to find that. So I began a search to learn what retirement really was for those living it. I wanted to know how they all were managing this—the good, the bad, and the ugly.

And so I listened to the stories of the "retired" and I wrote.

Fast-forward three years … My husband and I are now settled (?) in our new home, smaller in physical size and larger in emotional range. Our retirement process is in full swing, and the reality is not at all what we expected. Our days are good and bad, happy and sad, contented and unsettled. We know we made the right decision *for us.* There are days when we miss our other home and lifestyle, but for the most part, we are comfortable where we are. We've made our choices, and we are settling in to our latest adventure.

What follows is a compilation of multiple conversations with a wide variety of people. Each person shared openly their retirement experience. They shared their planning processes, their feelings as they entered this new stage of their lives, and their reflections on the choices they made to be "retired." They shared their panic and their ecstasy. They offered advice to those who will follow them into retirement. There is laughter and sadness in each personal story. I hope you enjoy the stories and the information helps you on your retirement journey.

- For those of you loving your retirement experience, I hope this book validates the choices and plans you have made to get where you are.
- For those of you who are dreading this next phase of your life, I hope this book lets you know that you are not alone in that dread and gives you some direction for making your own decisions.
- And for those of you just beginning to consider retirement, I hope these stories offer you an opportunity to explore the many possibilities you have before you.

I hope the book in total offers you some guidance on making *your own* decisions and living in *your* retirement with comfort and enjoyment.

In all cases, I hope this book brings a smile to your face as you walk through this next adventure ... and you find your own answer to *What Do I Do Now?*

Enjoy.

Jeanne
December 2020

With Thanks ...

Only with the candid input from all these
people was this book possible.
I thank them all sincerely.

Claudia and Herb	Jim
John	Len
Tricia and George	Glenn
Yona and Ed	Linda and Charles
Evelyn and Ted	Diane and Bill
Joseph	Joanne and David
Harriet and Steve	Fran and Bill
Peter	Matt
Jeff	

and Debbi Hines, without whom this book would not have been finished, who went over each line, formatted every page, and made the editing process painless (relatively) and always fun. Editor, contributor, and friend, Debbi keeps me on track and organized (more or less). Thank you seems inadequate and yet it says it all ... *thank you.*

Retirement Is ...

Not being responsible every day.

No longer going to a job with a salary.

Exhilarating!

Having the freedom to pick and choose what to do with your days.

Not having to go to a fixed work.

Having your own time schedule.

Stopping what you were doing—you know, all the daily details.

Interacting more with people.

Hoping you can replace your activity with something else.

Absolute freedom!

Frightening!

Sad ~ a realization of your mortality.

Doing what you want to do when you want to do it.

Relief from all responsibilities.

Enjoying your hobbies and grandchildren.

Losing the stress you felt before.

Not having to work and still having money and time!

Not having to get up and go to work!

Liberating because you construct your own schedule and get to choose where to invest your time and energy.

Not having a schedule, being stress-free, and being free to do whatever in your own time.

Sex at two in the afternoon.

Not having enough time to do everything you want to do!

PART I
PREPARING

Decisions, Decisions, Decisions

What Do I Want to Be When I Grow Up?

Do I Have To?

But I Don't Want To!

It's paradoxical that the idea of living a long life appeals to everyone, but the idea of getting old doesn't appeal to anyone.

———

Andy Rooney

What Do I Want to Be When I Grow Up?

Remember when you were a child and the grown-ups in the room would bend down and ask, "And what do you want to be when you grow up?" What a ridiculous question. If you were like me, you smiled coyly and answered inanely, "Fireman, policeman, teacher, astronaut." You would just say anything to the adult so you could get away. Then as you got older, you began to really think about it. *What* do *I want to be when I grow up?*

In his article "How to Know When You Are Grown Up." Paul Chernyak, LPC wrote:

> In general, being grown up indicates that you've evolved into a new stage in your life in which you take your career, relationship, and future more seriously. At the very least you have more concern for your future needs …

We are not talking chronological age. We are talking about emotional age and needs.

As you get older chronologically, you are faced with the reality of needing to do something that is satisfying and invigorating and that pays your bills. You have been growing up all your life. There were

1

no other options. As you aged, you needed to care for yourself and possibly others. The only way to do that was to work at something that would earn you the resources you could use to live the life you wanted. Growing up required an investment in time and effort. The return on that investment was measured in money and recognition.

At this point in your life, we are assuming that those needs are met. Now you have to ask yourself, what do I really want?

Now you have the opportunity to do something that may not be attached to money/rewards. As a grown-up, you have transitioned from what you *need to do* to what you *want to do* to have a life.

Now you can grow into whoever you want to be and do what you want to do without limits. Nothing is out of reach now.

The only limits you have are those you put on yourself.

Peter's Story

Think Peter Pan, J. M. Barrie's storybook character who chose not to grow up. The Peter in this story is a real-life boy who never thought about growing up. He never asked himself what he wanted to be when he grew up, because he had no intention of doing grown-up things. "I never thought I'd have to."

Peter's young life was comfortable and directed by his parents. "In my family, when your parents told you to do something, you did it." Peter's life was fun. He worked in his father's factory, played sports in high school, and followed his brother to college where he studied political science and psychology. He even followed his brother into the Air Force. "Life was fun. I had no direction, and I liked that."

After graduation, he bummed around the country doing various jobs. However, six months after graduation, he was obligated to fulfill his contract with the Air Force. He was stationed at an airbase where he was told he was good fighter pilot material. While in training to be a fighter pilot, he decided that he had no reason to read the training manual. He recalled, "It was easy to fly." He was on a path to wash out of the Air Force.

To be continued …

And now, it's your turn. Ask yourself:

- What do I *need* to do to feel alive?
- If there were no limits on what I could do, what would I do?
- Which of my dreams can I pursue now?
- How do I want to enjoy myself, find satisfaction in my life, and fill my days?

Half of our life is spent trying to find something to do with the time we have rushed through life trying to save.

———

Will Rogers

Do I Have To?

The answer to this question is yes. You have to grow up as in growing older. Growing older is not an option (sorry about that). Growing up, however, is a choice. Growing up in this sense is all about doing and being, and there you have a choice.

Some people don't choose to grow up in the sense of the doing and being. They manage to make it through life with little or no responsibilities, so for them, growing up is optional.

Remember, retirement is optional too. You don't have to retire. You can continue to work at a job for as long as you want until you are too tired, unhappy to keep going, or satisfied with your life as it is. I found that for most people, there was a sudden epiphany. One day they realized that they were done with this daily work "thing." It was like that door slammed shut on their work life, and as the saying goes, a large window opened to a view of a new/different life.

Remember that you are retiring from a job, not from your life. The rest of your life is ahead of you. There are so many ways to describe this:

- You are beginning a new adventure.
- You are writing a new chapter in your life story.
- You are adding more value to the world.

You have options. Remember, you make your own retirement.

5

Peter's Story, Continued

Peter was now officially in the Air Force. On the one hand, he realized when you're in the service, you have responsibilities, so you have to grow up. On the other hand, he thought, *I'm not going to die, and I'm not going to grow up.*

Peter had to make a choice: follow through on his commitment to the Air Force or allow himself to be washed out of the service. Without realizing what he was doing, Peter talked himself through his own pros/cons list. Peter's internal pros/cons list went like this:

Pros

- The Air Force is like my parents: they tell me what to do, and I do it. I'm OK with that.
- I get to do fun things, go to cool places, and get paid for it.
- I'm pretty good at this.
- Flying jet planes is fun.

Cons

- None that I can think of.

Peter was as grownup as he wanted to be. He realized that in the Air Force, he was "really doing it right instead of floating through." Peter made a decision to "grow up" and still have fun. He flew phantom jets for the Air Force for the next six years.

To be continued …

And now, it's your turn. Ask yourself:

- What does work mean for me?
- How can I be a grown-up and still have fun?
- How open am I to unexpected opportunities?

I haven't quite got the hang of this retirement thing.

———

Walter Cronkite

But I Don't Want To!

OK! You don't have to. Just like everything else in life, you have a choice. You can retire or not retire. You can choose how you retire. This is your life. You have choices. You make your own decisions.

Let's be realistic. Growing older, or aging if you prefer, is not an option so stop fighting the inevitable. You have been aging since the day you were born. You are aging right now as you read through this. Aging is an indisputable fact of living, and although aging does come to an end at some point, that point is not today.

Life is a journey. Every year you live, you are moving in a direction—sometimes forward, sometimes backward, and sometimes sideways until one day you realize your road has forked and you have to make a decision. What choice will you make?

If you choose to retire, you have options. You can quit your job, you can work part time, or you can continue working as you are now.

You don't have to retire. For some people, retirement is an organized, calculated process. For others, it just happens: a smooth segue into the next phase of life. For others, it happens unexpectedly. For others, it never happens, because they love what they do. The important thing is to respond to your personal wants and needs and adjust your life accordingly. Whatever you choose, make sure it's fun.

There is no formula to create that "perfect retirement." No retirement is the same. Your retirement is what *you* want it to be. You get to choose how you want to travel down that next road. You are in control really.

Make a decision. Get moving into the next chapter/adventure/phase of your life. It's OK. You can do this.

Peter's Story, Continued

Peter completed his obligation to the Air Force and returned to civilian life. He decided to "take a breather" before he considered going to work. He lived with his parents for a short time, ran a small commercial fishing operation by himself, and then travelled around the country, spending time with college friends because "staying in touch with old friends is staying young."

After several months, Peter decided he needed a job and interviewed to work as a pilot for Delta Airlines. They hired him within a week of the interview. However, he decided he didn't want that job and instead referred a friend, who was hired.

Ultimately, Peter accepted a position as an actuary, company salesman, and pilot for their company jet (a typical Peter Pan jump). He did well there and took over the company several years later. Shortly after taking over the company, he created the company he still owns.

Peter is not retired. He is just "not working too hard." He manages his company from the retirement village where he lives. His direction now is to begin phasing himself out of the company while ensuring that there is someone in line to manage the company and give his employees the security they need to live their own lives.

None of Peter's "work" was really planned. He never "decided" to grow up. He will tell you that he's still not grown up, although he is responsible and mature enough to continue managing his company at the age of seventy-nine.

His advice to you is "whatever you choose to do, make it fun, because then you are not really working and won't have to retire."

And now, it's your turn. Ask yourself:

- What are the policies for retirement at my work? Age limit? Financial ceiling? Tenure?
- Can I restructure the job that I have now such as job sharing, part time, or a compressed schedule?
- How can I add value to my world in a different way?
- How do I want to enjoy myself, find satisfaction in my life, fill my days, and have fun?

PART II
ACCEPTING

Moving Forward

Do I Move or Stay Put?

What Do I Do about the Family?

How Do I Shift Gears?

The best way to find what we really need is to get rid of what we don't.

———

Marie Kondo

Do I Move or Stay Put?

What is "home" to you? Is it your place of residence, or is it a state of mind?

Home. What picture comes to your mind when you hear that word "home"?

- Cozy nights in front of a fireplace?
- A safe haven from a storm?
- A family dinner at the table?
- Comfort, laughter, and warmth?

In the movie *The Quiet Man,* Maureen O'Hara's character knows she is home when she has "all my things about me." I absolutely understand that. Without my antique secretary and my piano, my home would be only a house.

It's true that our "home" is more than a brick-and-mortar structure that holds our things. Our home contains the memories of our life: laughter, tears, conversations, board games played on the floor, food prepared by many hands in the kitchen, music, and dancing. All those memories attached to our "things" make it our home.

I picture my home with the noise and confusion of little ones unwrapping gifts under the Christmas tree, watching my daughter and her bridesmaids prepare for her wedding, sharing overnights with my grandchildren, and spending quiet evenings on the deck in front of the fire pit. All the memories of my home are satisfying and calming, and the location doesn't matter. What matters is the feeling that I belong there.

As life moves along, the time comes when we realize that our memories are always with us, but our physical home has become more than we can handle by ourselves. The yard work takes longer to finish and is exhausting. The house cleaning can't be done in a day. The usual maintenance has gone from "I can do that" to "who can I call to do that?"

And now you began to ask yourself, do I move or stay put?

If I Move
- How large a house do I want/need?
- What do I do with my things?
- What advantages do I have if I move?
- What's the worst thing that could happen if I move?

If I Stay
- How will I manage this house?
- Who can I hire to do the yard work, cleaning, and maintenance work?
- What advantages do I have if I stay put?
- What's the worst thing that could happen if I stay?

Jim's Story:

Jim worked in the information technology (IT) services industry as a professional development trainer. Translation: Jim was a teacher of interpersonal skills to people who designed, developed, and sold high-end software programs. His work involved teaching multilingual, multiethnic adults in a classroom setting. He was very good at his job and enjoyed it.

Having worked at this international company for a number of years, Jim was eligible for a sabbatical. Although he wasn't ready for retirement, he thought this sabbatical would be a good "practice run." He had never been away from work for more than a long weekend. During his sabbatical, he didn't think about work or check his email, and he looked over his bucket list. Surprisingly, he enjoyed this time.

Returning to work, Jim let his bosses know that he was ready to retire, allowing them time to fill his position. Every time he put deadlines on a project, another project was offered that would extend his deadline. In the meantime, Jim dreamed about retirement and where he would go.

Prior to his sabbatical, Jim thought retirement would be boring and he would be at loose ends. Instead, he found himself dreaming about what he would do during retirement. It took a year and a half for Jim to finally, and happily, retire.

Jim asked himself what he needed in a location. In Jim's case, his needs were clear. He needed access to continuous learning, arts, music, and theater, warm weather, available quality healthcare, and easy socialization. After researching on the web and visiting several locations, Jim and his partner settled in a fifty-five-plus community in North Carolina, close to several colleges that offered adult learning courses and was known for its museums, theaters, and music venues.

"The whole retirement process was a positive experience."

Jim's advice to you is to "get comfortable with yourself, and make sure you are in touch with what satisfies you."

And now, it's your turn. Ask yourself:

- Is this my last move?
- What do I need in where I live?
- What do I want in where I live?
- What can I afford in terms of housing?

And in the end, it's not the years in your life that count. It's the life in your years.

———

Abraham Lincoln

What Do I Do about the Family?

You have considered your options and made your decision to manage your next adventure.

You have gone through all the checklists and begun to move in a new direction.

You are comfortable knowing that this is the best decision for you. You have put yourself first. Remember, the most important person in your life is *you,* and this is *your* life.

Now it's time to let the family know about the changes that are coming. Remember that this is an emotional time for everyone and requires a well-thought-out conversation. Each person is dealing with their own emotions as they react to your news. At its best, the conversation can be complicated. When you are discussing life-changing decisions, the conversation can be downright painful.

It is important to remember, as in any conversation, the value of the conversation is more in the listening than in the talking. Since you are leading this conversation, you are in control, and you have the responsibility to listen more and speak less as everyone absorbs your news.

Your family worries about you. They worry about your health as they watch you change physically (ah, that gray hair and loss of height!). They notice the new limitations in

- your hesitancy to drive at night,
- your struggle to open jars and cans,
- your need for assistance in walking, and
- your general slowing down.

Your family members worry about themselves too. They are beginning to realize that life with you is finite, and that may scare them. Be aware of their concern and feelings, and let them talk. In the long run, they will come to understand the decision you have made benefits them too. Don't be surprised if your family doesn't support your decision fully. If they don't understand it, they need to know that this is your life, not theirs.

Debbi's Story

Debbi's parents, in their sixties, had been discussing moving to a nearby retirement village for years. "We'll move there in five to seven years," they would say. Debbi and her sister were very supportive of the idea, as they were familiar with the retirement village and happy their parents were making the decision before they really needed to. They loved the idea of their parents enjoying their retirement years in a place where they had friends and few house chores.

And then one day, Debbi's mom offhandedly mentioned that they had asked to be put on the list for openings in the retirement village. Debbi felt blindsided even though they had discussed this many times. Suddenly, Debbi was flooded with sadness as she thought about how much her four-year-old son thought of her parents' house as his second home. She wanted him to have more time in this house, more time to make memories with his grandparents! She wasn't ready to let go of this house and memories yet, and she burst into wracking sobs.

As Debbi was crying, her brain was logically reminding her that this was the right thing for her parents, and she was really proud of them for making this decision, but emotionally, she felt a great deal of sadness and loss. Debbi blubbered all this to her mom, who was certainly caught off guard by the emotional reaction. After a good cry between the two of them, they were able to talk about the new memories they would make in the new home, especially when there was access to a pool, tennis court, and spacious grassy areas to play in.

And now, it's your turn. Ask yourself:

- Do I want family to help me with this decision?
- How much information am I comfortable sharing with my family?
- How will I handle my family's response to my decision?

We must be willing to let go of the life we have planned so as to accept the life that is waiting for us.

——

Joseph Campbell

How Do I Shift Gears?

You were so excited to be able to drive (legally). It looked so easy.

First, you started the car. For some of us, that meant finding the starter. In my dad's 1949 Mercury, the starter was on the dashboard, a button to push. You also needed to adjust the choke, a knob on the other side of the dash. Then you turned the key. The engine roared to life and you had to listen until it sounded "right." Then you could push in the choke, and you were ready to move.

On the Mercury, the gearshift was on the steering column. You had to move it in an H motion: up for first, down for second, up, over, up again into third, and then down for fourth. Reverse was a whole different process.

Shifting into first gear was a challenge: pressing in the clutch, then the accelerator, then easing off the clutch as you pressed more into the accelerator. It all involved coordination, timing, and courage.

There was a lot of stalling out as well, usually when going uphill. Those were the days before antiroll back. There was a quick look in the rearview mirror, hoping that the person behind you was far enough back that you could coordinate the brake/clutch/accelerator to move forward, and then you had to steer. At first, the learning curve was steep. In time, driving became second nature. You used all your limbs and concentration to steer the car. It was a whole-body exercise.

Life is the same way. As things change, you need to coordinate your whole body, your mind, and your spirit. There are days when you feel you are rolling backward, and you prepare yourself for the bump that you know is coming. There are times when life seems to have stalled for you, and you feel totally stuck, unable to move, just trying to restart. There are times when you know that you are heading in the right direction and the road is smoother.

William Bridges writes in his bestseller *Managing Transitions: Making the Most of Change,*

> It isn't the changes that do you in, it's the transitions. Change is situational. Transition is psychological. It is a three phase process that people go through as they come to terms with the details of the new situation.

In phase 1, you are leaving the past, acknowledging the ending of the life you know. In phase 2, you are balancing yourself between leaving your current life and reaching for the new one you have chosen. Phase 3 is actually the beginning of your life. Each phase is challenging and serves the purpose of ultimately moving you forward. Just like coordinating all your limbs and your concentration to drive the car, following through on your life decisions is a whole-body exercise. It's all about how you manage yourself through this transition.

Len's Story

Len's working life was multifaceted. He entered the Marine Corps as an officer after college graduation in 1962. After eight years of active duty, he entered civilian life while remaining in the Marine Corps Reserve until 1992. His civilian career included flying commercial helicopters in his own business, selling real estate, owning a retail store for a short time, and then working with a major insurance company as a director of commercial real estate until he left the business world in 2002. He doesn't feel retired. "I go from one project to the next. I am always busy. The only difference is now I can do what I want, where I want, and when I want. There hasn't been a hiccup between work and retirement.

I'm involved at church and with my grandchildren, attending lots of lacrosse games. The only thing I needed after my kids left home was life insurance. Once that was accomplished, I just kept moving on with my life."

Len managed his life's transitions by smoothly shifting gears.

And now, it's your turn. Ask yourself:

- How have I managed a life change in the past?
- How comfortable am I transitioning through new adventures?
- How comfortable am I with my final decision?

PART III
ADJUSTING
Living a New Life

What Will I Do?

I Will Learn New Things

I Will Have Fun ... or Not

Don't simply retire from something; have something to retire to.

———

Harry Emerson

What Will I Do?

Now there's a question for you. What will I do when I retire? In collecting these thoughts on retirement, the answers to that question range from "nothing" to "everything I've ever wanted to do."

The truth of the matter is retirement is the doorway to doing anything you have ever wanted to do and also never doing what you don't want to. Now that's a definition of freedom if I've ever heard one!

Harley Hahn, writer, philosopher, and humorist, writes:

> Freedom is a condition in which people have the opportunity to speak, act, and pursue happiness without unnecessary external restrictions. Freedom is important because it leads to enhanced expressions of creativity and original thought, increased productivity, and an overall high quality of life.

How do you like that? Retirement is an opportunity to experience freedom!

So how do you do that? Well, once again, it's time to write a list. This time, it is your "bucket list." To be clear, a bucket list is a number of experiences or achievements that a person hopes to have or accomplish in their lifetime, according to the *Oxford Dictionary*.

This is your opportunity to design a new life for yourself. This means you list *anything* you've ever wanted to do—no limits! It is a fun list, a list to address any fantasy you have ever had. Of course, you need to be specific. For example, if travel is on your list, then you need to add exactly where you want to go—not just Africa but the city of Timbuktu in Mali, north of the Niger River. If learning to play the piano is on your list, then you need to describe the type of music you will play and where you will play, such as Beethoven's Fifth Symphony at Carnegie Hall. Your list can have as many grandiose dreams and small goals as you want. It's your list of opportunities.

If you prefer staying local, you can get involved in your local university. There's a world of opportunities for you there. Remember the senior discount. You will find plays and dance performances, lifelong learning programs, and current events discussion groups. There are classes in memoir writing, painting, and yoga.

The local theater groups may offer classes in acting and musical performance. Many communities have choral and instrumental groups that always welcome new members.

Don't forget the museums! There are many programs and volunteer opportunities. You will be amazed how much you will learn and contribute to a museum.

Start checking off the items on your bucket list. Now is the time to enjoy this newfound freedom and do all you've ever wanted to do!

Claudia and Herb's Story

For Herb and Claudia, retirement gave them the freedom they had been looking for. Claudia retired first and involved herself with the crafts she had been doing all along. Her hobby of calligraphy evolved into a small business that she enjoyed on her own schedule. Herb had been working since he was twelve years old and was looking forward to living on his own schedule. His major concerns were financial. Once he felt secure with their financial arrangements, he was ready to enjoy living on his own schedule.

Herb and Claudia's bucket list had always been a work in progress and a part of their daily conversations. Their list included lots of travel. Specifically, they wanted to visit every state. Over the years, they accomplished that. They took day trips to explore new areas. They wanted a smaller house, one small enough to fit them and large enough to hold their family gatherings. Eventually they found a lovely townhome in a neat, wonderful, diverse community. Downsizing was not an issue, as there was "not a lot of stuff to sort through."

Now they keep busy volunteering and being with family. They travel through their area enjoying arts and crafts shows, local theater, and the uniqueness of their community. Now they have the freedom to do whatever "feeds their interests."

And now, it's your turn. Ask yourself:

- What do I need to keep busy, feel satisfied, have fun, and feel productive?
- What have I always wanted to try … just because?
- What can I do?

There is a fountain of youth: it is your mind, your talents, the creativity you bring to your life and the lives of people you love. When you learn to tap this source, you will truly have defeated age.

———

Sophia Loren

I Will Learn New Things

Retirement opens doors to new adventures. It presents you with opportunities to try something you've always wanted to do, expand your horizons, and add to your knowledge and abilities. Alison Winfield-Cheslitt, founder and DIY historian of the Good Life Centre in London, England offers ten reasons to learn something new:

1. To enhance your quality of life.
2. To reduce your stress.
3. To gain confidence.
4. To increase your knowledge (of anything you want!).
5. To improve your mental health (increasing your brain strength).
6. To socialize.
7. To be selfish (to have "me time").
8. To have fun (or FUNN—see the next chapter).
9. To set an example (for children and grandchildren).
10. To rediscover (yourself and the world).

M. K. Soni reminds us that we "are retiring from work not from life." So what do you want to try, and what's the worst that can happen if you do?

I can say from personal experience that learning to ride a motorcycle at the age of sixty-eight is definitely an adventure.

Taking watercolor classes with a trained artist after you retire is more than just fun. It is confidence boosting and personally powerful.

To plan and deliver a major gallery showing of your photographs is to set an example for those around you who look to you as a mentor, a sponsor, and a role model.

Here are some possibilities for learning new things, and most of them are free!

- Join the YMCA for fitness classes that include weight lifting to help maintain your bone strength, dancing classes for socialization, or craft classes.
- Volunteer to teach what you know within your community. You have years of knowledge and experience worth sharing.
- Take performing arts classes at local theaters: acting, singing, dancing, or performing.
- Auditing (free!) a course in just about any subject. These are available at many local universities and colleges.
- Attend adult night school classes in many subjects; check your local school districts for the list.

And remember you belong to that select group called senior citizens, and ask for the discount.

The most important part of your retirement is to do what you *want* to do. You are finished doing what you *have* to do. This is your "me time."

Glenn's Story

"I am a trucker. It's what I always wanted to be. Then I had a heart attack and was told not to drive. I was sixty-eight years old. I had never considered retiring and now I had no choice. I was empty. I had no purpose. I had to find something to do."

Glenn tried working a desk job at his old company. That didn't fit him. He did some part-time work driving a forklift for a transportation company. That was OK, but he still felt empty and bored. "I had to find something to do." Then he saw an ad on the internet for a senior citizen workout program at a local gym. "It will give me something to do."

The gym program was weight lifting for seniors. Glenn fell in love with it. "It was the best thing I ever did." He moved quickly through the program and then advanced his training. He was introduced to the world of competitive lifting. "I'm old, and if I die without doing this, then I'll die pissed off. I wanted to do this for me."

Glenn continued to work part time for a transportation company throughout this time, eventually working full time. He drives a sixty-five-thousand-pound forklift to move large steel beams onto large trucks. Glenn is seventy-four years old now and still drives that forklift.

Glenn forced himself to try something new. He did it for himself. By the way, he won several weight-lifting competitions and is a very happy man.

And now, it's your turn. Ask yourself:

- What do I want to do/learn?
- What can I share with others?
- What does my community have to offer me?

I don't want to retire. I still want to play.

———

Peyton Manning

I Will Have Fun ... or Not

If you've been paying attention, you'll notice that I have mentioned that retirement is an adventure, and this adventure is as fun as you choose to make it. To be clear, let's define some terms. The Microsoft Encarta dictionary defines adventure as "an exciting or extraordinary event or series of events." Let me add an additional definition for you. I prefer to use Project Adventure's* acronym FUNN, which means Functional Understanding Not Necessary. So we are talking about retirement as a FUNN adventure. Your retirement adventure can be filled with as many FUNN experiences/activities as you want. You are limited only by your own creativity. The choice is yours and does not need to make sense to anyone but you.

Charlie began retiring ten years before he actually retired. He enjoyed rescuing (collecting) things such as buildings, cars, and historical stuff. In particular, Charlie wanted to convert his old barn into a "party barn" so he could throw dance parties, so he did. That is definitely a FUNN adventure. By the way, the barn also holds an apartment on the second floor, and he rents space to others to store their cars in his barn. Charlie's FUNN adventure evolved into an income property!

Linda was an art teacher who was ready for retirement so she could travel, learn, and work in her studio. Today she does not have enough time to do everything. Her retirement allows her to follow her passion of creating art in her own studio, steps from her home.

Incorporating fun into your retirement is very important. The teachers I interviewed said it this way:

> "I didn't have to go to school in September."

> "I watched the first snowfall and rolled over in my nice, warm bed, knowing I didn't have to wait for the phone call telling me school was two hours' delayed."

My very favorite:

> "On the first day of school in September, I took my lawn chair to the thirteenth tee and waved at the school buses as they drove by."

Now that's FUNN everyone can understand!

---

* Project Adventure, Inc. is an innovative, nonprofit teaching organization and a respected leader in adventure-based experiential programming. For over forty-five years, PA has been committed to its mission of producing life-changing outcomes by facilitating transformative group experiences. PA provides a range of activities designed to build and enhance communication, often called ropes courses since the climbing, building, and designing/solving puzzles generally include ropes.

Joanne and David's Story

Joanne retired after thirty years of teaching school. Her retirement process was well organized. She reviewed and revised her financial situation. She spoke with her children. She contacted the school's human resources representative to work through all the paperwork the school district required for retirees. She was ready.

Her husband, David, as Joanne says, waited a year too long to retire. David says, "My father died at the age of sixty-two, and when I passed that age, I realized I'd forgotten to retire."

For both Joanne and David, retirement has been fun from the beginning. David has multiple hobbies and is comfortable reading and spending time at home. Joanne too has multiple hobbies and is comfortable being involved in church groups and book clubs. "We don't see each other a lot during the day, so when we come together, we have something to talk about. We missed that when we were both working, and now we have that time."

Joanne and David spend time with their children and grandchildren. The family gatherings are always fun, and of course, there is always FUNN at the beach.

And now, it's your turn. Ask yourself:

- What activity/adventure makes me happy?
- What would I like to try? (President George Bush Sr. was skydiving well into his nineties!)
- What FUNN do I want to have? (Remember, the sky is the limit. Sorry, I couldn't resist that.)

PART IV

ARRANGING

The Practical Side of Life

Can I Afford to Retire?

Organizing the Inevitable

The question isn't at what age I want to retire. It's at what income.

———

George Foreman

Can I Afford to Retire?

Can I afford to retire? Now there is a question that sets off major alarms in your head. So how about turning off the alarms by rephrasing the question. "How can I manage my money now so that I will have enough to start my retirement adventure?" OK, that's a better question, because now you can create the plan and take the steps to put it in motion. Let's break that down. Consider this:

Step 1: What plans have you made for managing money for your retirement adventure?

Ask yourself:
- How much money will I need for my living expenses?
- How much will I need for my "extras" such as travel expenses (most retirees do a large amount of traveling in their first few years), increased medical expenses, and increased costs for entertainment, restaurants, etc.?
- When should I start saving for retirement?
- What benefits do I have from my work that I can include in my plan?

Step 2: How will you know when you are ready to begin your retirement adventure?

Ask yourself:
- Do I feel comfortable that my retirement savings will outlast my retirement adventure?
- Have I made arrangements for my new life such as moving or staying put, medical coverage, wills, and funeral arrangements? (Prepaying your arrangements is strongly recommended.)

Step 3: What are you doing *right now* that is in line with your plan for your retirement adventure?

Ask yourself:
- Do I have a financial advisor who fits me and understands my needs, one I am confident will guide me through this adventure while I remain in control?
- Do I understand the benefits I will receive from my work when I retire?
- Have I decided when to take Social Security?
- Do I have a savings plan in place?

Step 4: What do you need to do *right now* to work on your retirement adventure plan?

Ask yourself:
- Am I saving money (any amount will do) on a regular basis?
- Do I have all my papers in order and easily accessible (wills, health care directive, etc.)?
- Have I let others know where those papers are along with the names of my financial advisor and lawyer?

Step 5: What will you let get in your way of living your retirement adventure?

Ask yourself:
- Am I saving monies on a regular basis?
- Am I trying to manage these affairs on my own?
- Am I waiting too long to start this process?

Did you notice that there is common thread in all these steps? Hopefully you picked up on the concept of saving your money. Saving money is difficult for some people and comes naturally to others. In either case, it is a necessity if you want to be able to retire from your job. Remember, you will be retiring from a job, not from your life. In fact, your life will move into an amazing retirement adventure if you plan and save starting now.

Bill and Diane's Story

Bill and Diane both came from typical, middle-class families. They met in college and married after graduation. They were both teachers in a large, middle-class suburban school district. Although they didn't know it at the time, they were planning for their retirement from the day they started their first teaching jobs.

Saving was not a top priority for them at the beginning. Raising two sons on teachers' salaries was a challenge, to say the least. However, during that time, they followed certain rules. They did not live beyond their means. The credit cards they used were paid off on time. They were never deep in debt. In the beginning, their money was spent on the necessities of maintaining a home and raising their children. They were able to put their sons through college and then concentrate on themselves.

Bill and Diane readily admit they are both self-disciplined and good planners with a financial mindset. They saved, and they used their savings cautiously. Occasionally they had to use their savings to pay for large items. They then paid that money back into their savings. They planned ahead for their retirement. They connected with a financial advisor who guided them toward achieving their goals. They stayed informed on their school district's pension plans. Bill retired after thirty-five years of teaching, and Diane retired after twenty-six years.

Now they are enjoying their retirement. Their bills are the basics: utilities, insurances, taxes, and food. They keep track of all expenses and income so they know at any time where their money is. More to the point, they are enjoying their life as they spend their retirement money while they are healthy enough to enjoy their adventures.

And now, it's your turn. Ask yourself:

- What are my bills?
- What is my income?
- What do I really need to live?

**When I stand before G-d at the end of
my life, I would hope that I would not
have a single bit of talent left and could
say, I used everything you gave me.**

Erma Bombeck

Planning for the Inevitable

By now you are realizing that retirement requires substantial planning. You need to consider all your options and make your choices. This is your life, and you are in charge, right down to your last moments.

There is, of course, one more fact to consider. Your time on earth is limited. That's not a morbid statement. It is a fact of life, and with it comes one more thing to do before you can enjoy the retirement you have created. You need to plan your life celebration, because this is your life and you need to celebrate it in your own way.

Many funerals today are different from those you might remember. Today's funerals are arranged to be celebrations of life. They are customized to the wishes of the deceased and may include special locations (churches, backyards, country clubs, halls, or beaches), food, music, and requests for the participants to join in the celebration with memorable stories and laughter. These funerals are meant to encourage the sharing of memories. They are meant to honor the departed by festively celebrating the essence of that person. They are meant to capture the spirit of a life story so the living can heal. After all, funerals are for the living. They are a way to help the living grieve their loss and honor their loved one. Funerals are a gift from the departed to the living. When you look at funerals from this perspective, you realize that funeral directors are event planners for the living.

As with any event planning, a life celebration requires you to consider what type of service you want, where you want your life to be celebrated, and how much you want to budget for this event. This is where a qualified funeral director fits into your planning. As an example, let me introduce you to a licensed funeral director and certified funeral celebrant who is the owner of multiple funeral homes and crematories. Through personal experience, he understands grief and has an innate ability to support the living through that process. At the same time, he knows how to honor each individual by telling their story, their way. He is professional, empathetic, and knows how to put the fun in funeral. You need to find the "right" funeral director with whom you are comfortable (that means speaking with several different directors) and who will help you write your life story and plan your celebration.

Talk to your loved ones, and tell them exactly what you want. At this point, nothing is off limits. This is your life and your celebration. Give your family and friends the opportunity to relive the fun you all had together.

Will and Ham's Story

Two brothers, both highly organized, accomplished, and fully prepared for this next life adventure … sort of.

Ham had been down this road many years ago when he was preparing for military combat and was required to set his affairs in order—just in case.

Will had prided himself on his organizational skills as a high-level professional. His work required him to plan ahead and keep his papers in order—just in case.

They were alike in many ways, and yet, when their time came, their different personalities revealed themselves in the preparations they had made for their last adventure.

Will was well into his eighties when his wife of fifty-plus years was struck with Alzheimer's disease. Her physical health had been failing for several years, and she had expressed to Will her wishes for an end-of-life celebration. He was not in total agreement with her wishes; however, he put her things in order legally and financially. He was prepared to manage her passing.

As often happens, life took an unexpected turn. His passing came unexpectedly while she was in stage 3 of Alzheimer's. Will had been prepared for her passing. He was not prepared for his own. Now their children had to manage his final arrangements. As you can imagine, the process was sometimes chaotic and felt incomplete and unsatisfying to them. They were never sure if the arrangements they made were what he wanted for himself.

Ham was in his late seventies when his physical health began to decline. The arrangements for his life celebrations had been carefully and meticulously laid out many years before. The preparations he had to make now were to finish his financial arrangements for his family. He worked diligently to accomplish that while he was still capable. Ham's celebration was everything he wanted it to be. He had listed timelines, locations, and ceremonies. He wrote lists and letters and communicated it all to his family. His family was comforted and satisfied with his life celebration, knowing they had followed through on his every instruction.

The lessons here are obvious.

1. Decide what you want for your life's celebration.
2. Write down what you want in detail.

3. Tell those you trust to follow through on your requests.

4. Give your loved ones the gift of knowing they have honored you.

And now, it's your turn. Ask yourself:

- Is my paperwork in order? Is it accessible?
- Have I described exactly what I want for my life celebration?
- Does everyone know my wishes who needs to know?
- Will my celebration be filled with joy and laughter so all the participants can remember the way they shared those special moments in my life?

And sometimes you just know it's time to start something new and trust in the magic of beginning.

———

Unknown

Epilogue

And So I Retired ... Sort Of

The day we bought our new (and much smaller) house in the continuing care community where we had chosen to spend the rest of our life was a sad day for me. Our new reality hit me hard. My feelings were running amok. I felt sad, angry, frustrated, lonely, and old. *Yuck!* I didn't like any of those feelings. Our life's road was heading in a finite direction.

> Maybe we had made the wrong move.
> Maybe we were rushing down this road.
> Maybe we should have stayed where we were.

It was time to revisit the pros and cons list we had made when we first started this journey. Our list looked like this:

Pros: The benefits of moving to continued care community	Cons: The negatives of moving to continued care community
- Maintenance free living	- We like to do things ourselves
- Close to family	- Community living/always lived in a single home
- Fits our budget	- House is smaller
- In our neighborhood	

As we looked at our list, we realized that the pros were strong and the cons could be managed. We are adaptable people. More to the point, we had to make this decision now before someone else would make it for us. We had plenty of time ahead of us, and it was important for us to be in control of our lifestyle. We understood that we were transitioning into a different lifestyle. We knew this was the first step toward our retirement, and the first step is always the hardest, the most comprehensive, and the most challenging. We asked ourselves, "If not now, when?"

Dian Griesel, author of *Silver Disobedience* writes:

> Retirement only means it is time for a new adventure. Let's look at some statistics: 50% of the population in the US as of 2017 is over the age of 50. About 10,000 reach retirement age every day, although most of us actually work well past 65. 45% of the Silver Disobedience population considers themselves entrepreneurial and is considering starting new businesses in their retirement while others are opting for travel and other forms of recreation.

So where do you think you are?

Have you created a lifestyle so you can say with certainty that "there was no hiccup between working and retirement"?

Are you struggling with the "I'm supposed to" theory of retirement? You know, "I'm supposed to retire when I'm sixty-two-sixty-five-seventy"; "I'm supposed to stop working at my job"; "I'm supposed to stay home and live simpler"; "I'm supposed to travel, move in with my children, downsize"; etc. Don't listen to the "I'm supposed tos"!

Are you doing what you love?

Do you love what you're doing?

Keep doing whatever elements of your job you enjoy, and stop doing what you don't enjoy.

Start something new.

My husband is still working in a profession/vocation he has loved all his life. I still coach executives in communication and leadership skills, and I write, which is something I've always wanted to do. I set my own schedule. We still enjoy every sunset on our deck in the new backyard just as we did before.

I admit there are times when I struggle with the emotions of this major life change. I am still adjusting.

This is what I am doing now. This new adventure is underway and life is good.

And now, it's your turn. Ask yourself:

So what do I do now?
And if not now, when?

ADVICE, LAST THOUGHTS, AND RESOURCES

Advice and Last Thoughts
from the Already Retired

Resources

I hope you still feel small when you stand beside the ocean
Whenever one door closes I hope one more opens
Promise me that you'll give faith a fighting chance
And when you get the choice to sit it out or dance
I hope you dance

———

Lee Ann Womack

Advice and Last Thoughts from the Already Retired

Part I: Preparing: Decisions, Decisions, Decisions

- What is old? At my age, I still have dreams.
- People who are defined by their job may not be happy in retirement.
- I'm not adding value to the world.
- It's a weird feeling getting up without something to do.
- If you don't have a purpose, you don't have life.

Part II: Accepting: Moving Forward

- I thought I would volunteer in my area of expertise. It turns out that volunteering is not always fun.
- Recognize the little things that retirement gives you.
- I was surprised at how active I became.
- Give yourself space to allow the unexpected to come in.
- If you've got a dream go do it! Your bucket list is real. Do it now. You don't know what's around the corner.
- You've got to have other interests.
- I just segued into retirement. It was a gradual move.
- Retirement is an evolution.
- Should have downsized sooner.

Part III: Adjusting: Living a New Life

- Learn to say no or you can get overwhelmed volunteering.
- Always have two TVs so you each can watch what you want without arguing.
- Stay involved until the very end.
- Reinvent yourself. Start something new.
- When I retire, I plan to travel, continue my education, live closer to family, be more physical, relax more, and run a marathon.
- How to travel when you are older:
    - Plan, plan, plan
    - Realize your physical limitations and stamina
    - Consider many smaller trips versus big ones
- I became restless and felt the need to give back. How was I going to contribute? I needed to serve others so I joined the Rotary. Now I am teaching at temple, spending more time with my grandchildren, and just living my life. I found that opportunities presented themselves for me to learn more about myself.
- Husband: The best thing about retirement is being able to spend more time with my wife.
- Wife: We needed to negotiate being in the house at the same time.
- Retirement gave me a list of "things to do" instead of a "to do" list. There's not enough time to do the things I want to do, and I don't feel pressured to do things.
- Find your passion.
- Be passionate about something.
- We had to adjust the way we argued since we had more time together.
- Don't slow down. Keep going to the end.

Part IV: Making This Work Practical Side of Life

- We want to spend this time and money when we can with our health, because the day could come when we can't and the money won't mean anything.
- It took me six months to fully understand I would survive.
- In terms of money, you have several choices: save it—for how long? Or spend it—on what?
- You know the phrase "you can't take it with you." Well, you can't.
- A heart attack at an early age totally changed my life. Health care is a hidden cost of retirement. I should have saved more.

Resources

Pros and Cons List

The Pros and Cons List is a technique I've used for many years to help me logic through a decision. Here's what you do. Divide an 8 x 11 inch piece of paper in half lengthwise, giving you two columns.

Column #1 is the Pros Column where you will list all the positive results you will gain by making this move/decision. This move/decision is not necessarily just a physical move. Rather it is a move to a different type of life (your retired life).

Ask yourself:

- What will I gain from making this move/decision*?
- What will this move/decision* allow me to do that I can't/ don't want to do now?
- What will be the return on this new investment in me?

Column #2 is your Cons Column where you will list all the things that are wrong (in your mind) with making this move/decision.*

Ask yourself:

- What is the worst thing that can happen to me if I do this?
- What will I lose in making this move/decision*?
- How miserable will I be when I do this?

* This move/decision is not necessarily just a physical move. Rather it is a move to a different type of life (your retired life).

Now this list doesn't happen at one sitting. This is a list that takes time to complete. I suggest you carry it with you and add to it as you go through your day.

Remember this is *your* list. You can add, subtract, and rearrange as many times as you like until you are comfortable with all the items on your list. Now put it aside and don't think about it for at least three days. Then reread it, and ask yourself "Do I have to make this move/decision?" What's your answer?

Pros: The benefits of making this decision	Cons: The negatives resulting from this decision
1.	1.
2.	2.
3.	3.

Downsizing

Downsizing is a requirement for making a life change whether you are moving or staying put.

Downsizing is the process of simplifying your living without losing your memories. It is a physical act that is encased with emotion.

Downsizing has major benefits for both your home and you.

Downsizing does not happen overnight. It is a process.

Before you downsize, take photos of each room so you can (1) revisit that room as it is and (2) inventory those things as you decide what to keep.

Suggested Steps:[1]

1. Work on one room at a time, not the whole house!
2. Set a time limit of no more than two hours at the beginning. You do have tomorrow. Honest.
3. Look around the room, and sort the items in your mind as you place them somewhere where you can see them all, asking yourself:
   "Do I use this? How often?"
   "Do I need this? Can I live without this?"

4. Create three piles:
   - I will keep this.
   - I will donate this.
   - I will trash this.
   - Once you have put the items in their piles, *do not* look back.
   - Put your keep items away where they belong.
   - Take your donated items to their destinations (check the list in the references section).
   - *Throw away* your trash items *now*.

5. Congratulate yourself on a job well done!

---

[1] There are several recommendations on the downsizing process, and if you want there are companies that specialize in helping you to get this done. You don't have to do it all yourself.

Books

Albom, Mitch. 1997. *Tuesdays with Morrie*. New York: Doubleday.

Bridges, William. 2003. *Managing Transitions: Making the Most of Change*. Cambridge: Da Capo Press.

Cameron, Julia, and Emma Lively. 2016. *It's Never Too Late to Begin Again/Discovering Creativity and Meaning at Midlife and Beyond*. New York: TarcherPerigee.

Duckworth, Carolee, and Marie Langworthy. 2013. *Shifting Gears to Your Life and Work After Retirement*. Sherrills Ford, NC: New Cabady Press.

Griesel, Dian. 2019. *Silver Disobedience Play Book*. Pittsburgh: Dorrance Publishing.

Hume, Sally Balch. 2017. *Get the Most Out of Retirement*. Washington, DC: American Bar Association.

McClellan, Jeanne Taylor. 2018. *The Times of My Life: A Journal of Personal Discovery*. West Grove, PA: jmcclellanpublishing.

McPhelmy, Lynn. 1997. *In the Checklist of Life: A Working Book to Help You Live and Leave This Life*. Rockfall, CT: Aaip Publishing Company.

Morris, Virginia. 2018. *Talking about Death Won't Kill You!* Toronto: ECW Press.

Schultz, Kenneth S., PhD, with Megan Kaye and Mike Annesley. 2015. *Happy Retirement—The Psychology of Reinvention/A Practical Guide to Planning and Enjoying the Retirement You've Earned*. New York: DK Publishing.

Sher, Barbara. 1994. *I Could Do Anything If I Only Knew What It Was. New York, NY:*Dell Publishing

Internet

www.aarp.org

www.harley.com/harley-quotes/uc1-quotes.html. Hahn, Harley. 2020. "What is freedom?"

www.wow4u.com/mksoni. Soni, M. K., n.d

www.talkofalifetime.org

www.thegoodlifecentre.co.uk/?s=learn+something+new+every+day The Good Life Centre. 2020. "10 Reasons to Learn Something New Every Day."

www.wikihow.com/Know-when-You-Are-Grown-Up%3famp=1 Chernyak, Paul. 2019. "How to Know When You Are Grown Up".

Movies (for the fun of it)

Last Vegas
The Bucket List
Red
Second-Hand Lions

About the Author

Jeanne Taylor McClellan is the owner of J. Taylor Consulting, a consulting firm located in Chester County, Pennsylvania. Jeanne is a transformative coach and management consultant with extensive experience in organizational effectiveness, people development, and team building. She holds degrees in education and adult counseling and certifications in adventure training and forensic psychology.

Jeanne has been working since she was fifteen years old: from waitressing to retail sales to office assistant to per diem and long-term substitute teaching to developing her own counseling office to leading organizational development initiatives in corporate settings. Since establishing J. Taylor Consulting in 1997, Jeanne has designed and delivered people focused developmental strategies in multiple organizations nationally and internationally. Today, Jeanne concentrates on coaching managers and executives as they work to transform themselves professionally and personally. Jeanne schedules her work life to fit into a schedule of exercising, traveling, spending time with family and friends, and of course, writing.

Jeanne Taylor McClellan is the author of three books:

The FUNctional Facilitator: Because Attitude Is Everything
An essential guidebook with techniques for facilitating, coaching, and leading groups

Sea Stars: Stories of Hope, Happiness, and Helping Hands
A variety of short stories that illustrates you should never underestimate the impact that your words and actions have on the lives of others

The Times of My Life
A self-guided journal for remembering and recording the events and people in your life (a great activity for retirement!)

Jeanne and her husband live in Chester County, Pennsylvannia. They have five daughters and six grandchildren.

Jeanne would love to hear about your retirement adventures. She can be reached through her websites: www.jtaylorconsulting.com and www.jeannetaylormcclellan.com.